A to Z

of

Loving Work

Andrew Horder

Foreword by

Nick Williams

Author of 6 books, including *The Work We Were Born to Do*

First Published 2011 by Busy Fool Press
Revised Edition Published 2016

ISBN number 9781539314011

Copyright © 2016 Andrew Horder

www.Joyful-Genius.com

Busy Fool Press
Business Strategy Solutions Ltd
115 Lumley Road, Horley, Surrey, United Kingdom RH6 7JG

This book is dedicated to my wonderful wife and soul-mate Daniela, who gives me the inspiration and the freedom to create and develop my ideas .

What readers are saying:

"This book is a new lexicon for how to build and run a business you love. If you just read and act on one of these chapters a week, in half a year you will be operating on a whole new level. This is a veritable A to Z of business wisdom. By absorbing and combining these gems into new ways of being and doing, a whole new language is open to us for how we can run our lives and businesses."
Tom Evans, Author of Flavours of Thought & The Art and Science of Light Bulb Moments
www.tomevans.co

"If it's clarity, and direction with conviction that you want.....get the A to Z of Loving Work, and you'll never work another day in your life. You'll simply excel at what you love to do."
Fraser J. Hay, Marketing Consultant, Coach & Author www.theresultsacademy.com

"The A to Z of Loving Work is an essential focusing guide for those considering working for themselves or who have just taken the plunge."
Judith Germain, Leadership Consultant,
www.developing-leadership.com

"This is an extremely well-written book that takes an incredibly significant concept and makes it simple: if your work isn't fun, either it's not for you or you're not doing it right. I so whole-heartedly agree!"
Magic Friedman, The Heart Specialist,
www.magicfriedman.co.uk

1

"Andrew's relevant and clear case studies let all readers to make effective change fast, you will hit the nails squarely on the head and know why, as well as what, to do to get the results you want. I read lots of books and this one stands out as exceptional"
William Buist, Collaboration consultant, www.abelard-uk.com

"Thanks for this little gem Andrew. A nice balance of Why and How, in an easy, helpful style"
Stuart Kerslake, Fractional Finance Director
www.vfd.nextstep4me.co.uk

"Andrew's book is a great tool for learning to focus on why you do what you do. Whether you are working for a boss or working for yourself this book is full of practical advice and tools for improving your focus and direction. An Excellent book and highly recommended"
Sharif George, Founder, mycloudberry.co.uk

"An ABC opus; grand in its simplicity - and it's interactive, too!"
Benn Abdy-Collins, Transitions Mentor, www.transition.nextstep4me.co.uk

"Andrew's book is a massive step up from the self-help books that suggest success is easy if you just have the right mindset. This book focuses on the key thought processes you need and provides an impressive A-Z of what you need to do. At the end of each very readable chapter there are some key questions to help focus you on how you will get to love your work, your business and your career."
Mark Lee, "The most networked accountant in the UK" (AccountancyAge 2011) www.BookMarkLee.co.uk

Acknowledgements

The ideas in this book have been inspired (and sometimes directly borrowed) from a number of great friends, coaches, mentors, philosophers and thinkers who I've been fortunate enough to bump into over the years.

Nick Williams, with his Inspired Entrepreneur community, has been a great encouragement that it really isn't lunacy to believe we can all have work that we love and that inspires us. Another Nick, the lovely Nick Heap set me on the path with his three-word challenge: "Why not you?" after doing Core Process 2 for me. And I have to thank Nick for making me aware of Core Process, for training me to do it, and for his commitment and hard work in keeping it going. And Tom Evans has made a great contribution to the concept of 'Busy Foolery', in fact the name of one of my blogs "The Busy Fool" came from a conversation with Tom years ago.

I would never have met many of the people who have helped form my ideas, the Ecademy Blackstar Life members, if it wasn't for Thomas and Penny Power, founders of Ecademy. Particular Blackstars who have helped me formulate and promote my ideas include (in no particular order): Richard White, Fraser Hay, William Buist, Malcolm Tullett, Sharif George, Judith Germain, Colin Newlyn, Benn Abdy-Collins, Derek Bishop, Bryan Barrow, Chris Bose, Mark Lee, Fintan Galvin, Mike Turner, Phil Shepherd, Rory Murray, Alan Rae, Stuart Kerslake and Lis Cashin. These and many more have offered me support and guidance for which I am enormously grateful.

My amazing cover photo was done by the very talented headshot specialist John Cassidy, anyone who can make me look that good has to be worth a special mention!

My great friend Nicole Bachmann, with our (ir)regular chats over tea in Waterstones, has been a constant inspiration and reminder that I choose to live my life with outrageous joy.

Last, but by no means least, I owe enormous gratitude to my late grandfather Fred, my late father Mike, my remarkable mother Mary, and to my beautiful wife Daniela, without whose love, guidance, support and, above all, tolerance I could not have developed these ideas.

Thank you all.

Foreword by Nick Williams

Sadly, too few of us grow up being encouraged to think in inspiring ways about ourselves and the world of work. I wasn't. We are encouraged to think of work largely as an economic activity that allows us to make money and enjoy the remainder of our lives. At worst, we are taught that work is a necessary evil, a form of suffering to be endured, and that we just have to get used to that. That is so sad.

We aren't often taught about the tremendous gifts, talents, potential and possibilities that lie within every human being. We aren't always taught that work can be a joy, a tremendous way to express our gifts and talents in the world, a way to serve our fellow human beings, to tap into and express our potential and simply be happy.

But that *is* the potential of good work. Work that plays to our strengths and allows us to express the best of us. Our work can even be, as the philosopher Kahlil Gibran said so eloquently, "Our love made visible."

Andrew does a wonderful job of guiding you to re-imagine your work, and your place within your work. He gently invites you to bravely step into the world of self-awareness and ask the bigger questions that can lead you to your own happiness and fulfilment. He invites you to enquire into your best self and best qualities and see what you discover.

Believe there is greatness within you, believe that there are talents and gifts that are inside you itching to be expressed, and that you can find what is precious and unique about yourself. Believe that you are bigger than your fears and insecurities and doubts. Believe that you can create work around what you love and be well paid for doing what lights your heart up. You can. Believe it.

Nick Williams, author of six books including the best-selling *The Work We Were Born To Do* and co-founder of www.inspired-entrepreneur.com

London May 2011

Introduction

No doubt you are like all of us – you want to do something you love for a living. Life is far too short to spend half your waking hours doing something that doesn't bring you joy. Yet some-how, it is all too easy to slip off the path isn't it, to end up doing all sorts of work that you don't really choose, to become a Busy Fool?

I started writing this little book to provide other individuals finding it hard to focus on the work they love, other people in business finding themselves torn between making the money and enjoying life, in short, other 'busy fools' like me, with a guide to understanding all the many aspects of doing what you love for a living. And in the process, I found a number of ways I could improve my own working life, and get even more joy from making a living doing work I love.

My core focus for the last few years has been Focus. Getting business owners and entrepreneurs to focus on their best opportunities, the opportunities that they will enjoy doing and will get them where they want to go. Because it is that focus that creates results, giving enough attention to their core activities, that they love and will produce their success. It is clear to me that a major factor in how successful people are, is how much joy they find in their work. So I have made it my business to understand what makes work enjoyable for people in business, and to share that with those who need to know.

The book is written in the form of an A to Z, which means that it is not something that you have to read through from start to end. Each letter can stand on its own, so you can come back and re-read any of them individually and it will still make sense. And it is designed to be read in order the first time through, because the topics build on each other.

Some concepts are restated in a slightly different way – that is deliberate, and that should give you the clue that they're important. Don't make the mistake of thinking you've already read about this or that, and skipping over it – there is some-thing new in each letter.

I believe we are all holistic beings, we can only be truly successful if all aspects of our lives are full of joy. Work, in whatever form it takes for you, takes up a large part of our lives, so it is vital that you find a way to find joy in it because how you feel about your work will spill out into the rest of your life – you had better make it joyful!

The A to Z

"Nothing is really work unless you would rather be doing something else" James M. Barrie

"You've achieved success in your field when you don't know whether what you're doing is work or play" Warren Beatty

"When people go to work, they shouldn't have to leave their hearts at home" Betty Bender

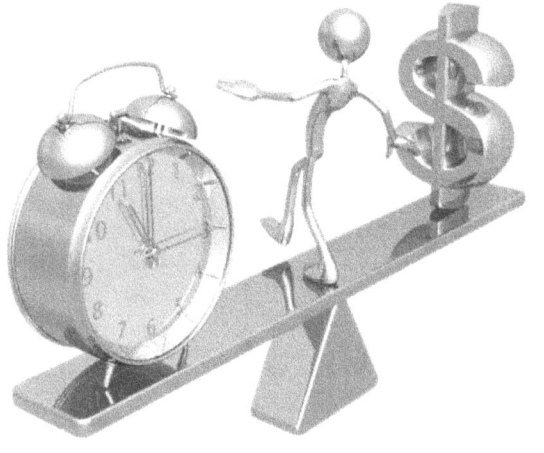

"To find joy in work is to discover the fountain of youth" Pearl S. Buck

"If you cannot work with love but only with distaste, it is better that you should leave your work." Kahlil Gibran

"Choose a job you like and you will never have to work a day in your life" Confucius

Action

If you want to love what you do for a living, and make a living doing what you love, you are going to have to take action.

I don't agree with the theory that if you just do what you love, the money will come. There is lots else that has to be right - a way of adding value for others by what you love doing, for instance, and a product or service that people want and will pay for. But actually "doing what you love for a living" starts with *doing*.

People need to know what it is that you do, and they want to see your passion. And they cannot do that if you are just thinking about it. Or worse, you are still planning, waiting to perfect your technique or your subject knowledge. Once you can do your thing better than most, or you know your subject more than most, it is time to start *do*ing it.

Unless you are already at the top of your field (in which case, what are you waiting for??), you are not going to be starting off charging 'guru' rates, so why should you feel you have to give 'guru' performance? People are generally realistic - if they are paying £100 an hour, they expect competence, not brilliance.

So long as you know that what you deliver will be what they need and that it will be worth far more than they pay for it, do not let fear of not doing it quite right get in your way. Aim to give them more than they are paying for, just remember you really do not have to be 100% perfect.

Mark was a client some years ago, who had been thinking for some time about his idea of creating a network of specialist tax advisors. It was something he really wanted to do, but he was concerned about some challenges that might make it less than perfect. As we talked, he suddenly looked up from the analysis we were doing, and said "I just need to get on with this, don't I?"

So he did. It wasn't perfect straight away, and it took a while to get going – but get going it did. He soon had a good number of specialist advisors signed up, and a lot of potential clients for them. There were some early issues with the model, but it worked, and people were soon doing business on his platform. TaxAdviceNetwork.co.uk now has almost 30 specialist advisers across the UK and thousands of users of the website.

And Mark's work on that network eventually drew the attention of one of the largest providers of corporate networks, who invited him to join them to run some of their networks. He is now annoyingly delighted with the work he is doing.

Inspirational speaker Les Brown sums it up:

"You don't have to be great to get started, but you do have to get started to be great."

Exercises

What Actions are you putting off right now?

Where in your career or business is hesitation holding you back?

Who could help you to overcome your reluctance to act?

When do you find yourself hesitating to act?

How could you become more action-oriented?

"Even if you're on the right track, you'll get run over if you just sit there!"

Will Rogers

Busy Fool

There is a big difference between loving your work, and just doing lots of fun things during working time.

It is very easy to get drawn into all number of activities that don't really contribute to you doing what you love for a living. That might be 'interesting' projects that you get invited to join, or it might be tasks that no-one else wants to do.

It is very easy to convince yourself that all sorts of things are included in doing what you love for a living– especially if things are a bit slow in your own business, or your boss is putting you under pressure in a job. So you accept work that's not 100% work you love, but it is good enough; after all, you need the money or you need to keep the boss happy.

And then you get asked to do something similar, that's just a little bit farther away from your ideal. And that takes you yet further away from what you set out to do. Before you know it, your time is all taken up with work you don't really want to do, and you have no time to develop your ideal work.

You've become a Busy Fool!

It is all too easy to get yourself involved in all manner of exciting and interesting projects, any one of which could bring you riches - and to leave yourself with insufficient time to do any of them very well. And to flit frantically from one to another, desperately trying to find the time to make each one work – only to be frustrated and just spinning your wheels as none of them succeeds.

You've become a Busy Fool!

When I first left the corporate world I became a Busy Fool in both of the ways I describe above. I got involved in two fascinating projects – one creating an entrepreneurs' incubator service, and one based around helping corporate refugees to start up on their own. But they weren't well enough thought out, and the teams didn't have sufficient cohesion to survive the inevitable challenges. I spent hours and hours in meetings, travelling to meetings, working on proposals and on the phone with the others. They swallowed up enormous amounts of time, money, effort and resources, and they didn't create any meaningful results at all. I learned a lot on both of them, but neither was really right for me at the time.

And when things were a bit tight, I was asked to take on some Account Management work in an area I wasn't really familiar with. Which I did, and for a while it all went well. But the time I had to commit to it meant I couldn't do any work at all on my coaching model. Worse still, it interfered with some work I had taken on for a company I admired, to gain some experience of a particular area where I was a bit weak (see page "X" for why that can be a good idea). So the short term gain of a few extra pounds, and the desire not to upset someone in my network who was doing me a favour, actually cost me dearly in the long term, both in terms of my learning and in terms of enjoying my work.

B

Whether you are employed in a job or working for yourself, if you want to be successful at making a living doing what you love, it is essential that you define clear boundaries about what is and what is not part of 'me loving my work'. You have to know where to draw the line, when to say "No", when something you're considering doing is a valuable addition to your dream work and when it is just a distraction.

And the most important person you need to enforce those boundaries with is ... yourself!

Exercises

What are your major distractions right now?

Where do you find yourself most likely to diversify too much?

Who are the people who most ask you to go beyond your area of focus?

When do you feel most stretched from your core work?

What practical steps can you take to stay focused?

Clarity

To set yourself up to make a living doing what you love, you need to be completely clear on what it is, really, that you love to do.

Without that clarity, you will struggle to set appropriate boundaries for yourself and for others, and you will find it too easy to drift from your purpose. There are a vast number of ways to achieve this clarity, so I shall just share with you some of my favourites that I have used over the years, both for myself and with clients.

The first is to understand what your Values are, the things that are truly important to you in your life. The temptation is to look only at your career or business values, but in for best results you really need to be looking at your values for your whole life. After all, the whole objective of loving work is to make it so that what you do for a living is a vibrant, enjoyable and important part of your life.

To help with this, there is a 'values elicitation' audio available at www.opportunity-matrix.com/values - it's free, just sign up.

The next is to understand what you are doing when you are really at your best. Most of us have something that just comes naturally to us, that we intuitively know how to do well, that really lights us up when we do it. And often we don't value it because it is so easy for us, we really don't understand why others value us when we do it. If you have a coach, you will probably have already identified this.

The method I use is called Core Process (you can find more details at TheBusyFool.com), which uses storytelling to help identify what you have been doing when you have been at your absolute best. My Core Process is "encouraging potential" – so you can see why what I do for a living leads to me loving work.

When I first discovered my "Core Process", I was helping to run a small business, and consulting on Key Account Strategy. It was OK, but I felt that there was something 'bigger' I was supposed to be doing. Shortly after getting my Core Process I realised that I could adapt one of the models I was using to help people in business get more focused. As I got clearer on what really lit me up, what made me feel I was really living my purpose, I moved away from the Key Accounts work and began to focus on focus coaching. And specifically on getting people focused on doing what they love for a living.

Getting clear on what you love to do does not necessarily mean you have to change jobs. It is often quite possible to find ways to do the things you love within the context of what you are doing already. In fact, usually the reason why you took that job on is because you recognised, maybe unconsciously, that it would allow you to do activities that you can enjoy. The trick is to understand which parts you love to do, and attract more of those, and know which tasks or projects you would prefer to avoid.

You may have your own favourite ways to clarify what you really love doing. If not, ask your coach to help you, or try out one of my methods. If you are lucky enough to have a friend with whom you can be completely open and honest, and who will be totally with you, then you probably won't need a coach for this. Though in my experience, such friends are very rare indeed. The important thing is that you get completely clear on what "loving work" means for you. With that clarity you will find it so much easier to arrange your working life such that you do that every working day.

Exercises

What are your values?

Where are you truly at your best?

Who do you help most when you are in your flow?

When do you feel most certain about what you are doing?

How can you keep your work aligned with your values and talents?

Decisions

Decisions are much easier to make when you have clarity about what you are really trying to achieve.

And in the context of making a living doing what you love, knowing exactly what that is, and having a simple method to quickly decide which of your options is most likely to allow you to do that, is essential.

It is often said, in the success literature, that wealthy people tend to make decisions quickly, and change their minds rarely, while unsuccessful people hesitate for ages before making a decision, and then dither about actually putting it into practice. That is true to an extent, and there is more to it than simply making decisions quickly. A lot of unsuccessful people also make decisions quickly – they're just the wrong ones!

So how do successful people get to make the right decisions, and make them quickly? By doing their homework; there is no quick-fix, no silver bullet answer. They do the hard work to understand their market, their clients, their business, themselves – in fact everything that could make a decision a good one or a bad one. And here is their trick – they only do it once. They focus, so everything they learn can be re-used for their next decision.

And each decision is backed up with all their previous research, plus whatever they have learned since. They don't have to start their information-gathering from scratch every time. They do the work of figuring out the right work or business to be in, once. After that, it is just maintenance. So they have the information they need to make a confident decision quickly, without having to think about it too hard.

Where unsuccessful people go wrong is they skim the surface and then make bad decisions they later doubt, and feel they have to keep checking over and over. That is no way to enjoy your work – it detracts from the pleasure even of work you enjoy if you haven't put in the hours to know what you are doing in the first place.

When every decision you make comes with a doubt attached, you will find yourself always expecting to be 'found out'. Whenever I hear people saying they feel like they are a bit of a fraud, that sometime soon people are going to realise they have been making it up as they go along, I know they haven't put it the work required to make work a joy.

In my previous career in retail, I once took a job I was hopelessly under-qualified for. Even my staff had a better idea how to do the job than I did – and it wasn't the usual complaint of "I could do better than my boss", they really could! It was one of the worst years of my working life, because I really didn't know what I was doing. Eventually, what I had spent the previous year dreading happened, and the directors realised we had all made a horrible mistake. And I have never been so relieved to lose a job!

To be confident in your decisions, you need to put in the work to feel that you know what you are talking about.

Once you have done that, the work will start to feel easy, and to feel like it is not work at all. And you can't know enough about everything, so you will first need to put in the work to know what it is that you really want to do. There is no quick fix – all those successful people who seem able to make the right decision at the drop of a hat have worked hard to get to that point.

It is like I once heard stock market trainer "Aussie Rob" say – only lazy people work!

Exercises

What gets in the way of you making good decisions quickly?

Where do you find yourself having to revisit your decisions?

Who can help you get the information you need?

When do you have to make decisions without enough facts?

How can you increase the quality of your decisions?

Enjoyment-Performance Theory

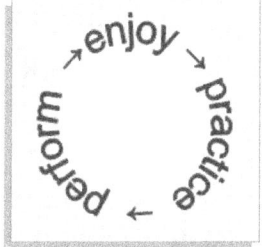

Enjoyment-Performance Theory comes from behavioural theory. Essentially it says that we perform better at tasks that we enjoy.

And we enjoy tasks we can perform well – that's why we can perform them well, otherwise we would never have done them enough to become practised at them. And because we enjoy them, and we do them well, we practice more – and become even better at them. And the virtuous circle continues ....

That rather begs the question why we don't all just stick to what we enjoy. The truth of it is, we generally do start off doing so – that is why we become good at it. It may not be what makes our heart sing, but on the whole most people start out in life doing things they enjoy, to some extent. For me, that was developing relationships with clients and analysing their needs so I could help them. Of course, it was wrapped up a role called "furniture salesman" in a department store. No-one was going to offer me a job as an 'analytical relationship-building helper', so I had to find a position that would benefit from my particular talent.

Then people get ambitious, and get themselves promoted, so they take on other stuff, that maybe they don't enjoy so much. I know I did; as I said, one of the worst years of my working life was the one I spent trying to be the manager of a department store. I learned loads, mainly about myself, but I absolutely did not enjoy it, and I certainly didn't perform well.

But, after all, I had to progress, didn't I? – it's not all about having fun, you know, it is serious stuff, this business lark!

Hmmm ...

Personally, my view is that there is something far more serious than business ... a little thing called **Life!** And you are doing yourself, and those who could benefit from your talents, a great disservice if you are wasting 40-plus hours a week on something that you are not enjoying, and therefore not performing to the very best of your abilities.

I've lost count of the number of times people have come to me complaining that they don't enjoy their work, yet still feel entitled to carry on taking their salary. That is acceptable if they are still producing the results they are getting paid for. But in so many cases, they admit when pressed that they are only doing the bare minimum, just enough to make sure they don't get sacked or don't lose the client.

The trouble is, taking that attitude to your work has an effect on you as well. If we enjoy what we do well, it is also true that doing something to less than your full ability will mean you enjoy it less. So it is hardly surprising that some people end up hating work when they are not throwing themselves into it 100%. So if you can't find a way to love what you do, you had better find a way to start doing what you love.

Anything else is a complete waste of your brilliance.

Exercises

What part of your work do you truly enjoy?

Where in your work do you feel you are having to do it?

Who would support you in wanting to enjoy your work more?

When does a need to be 'hard-working' show up in your work?

How can you get more joy in your daily work?

"Just as your car runs more smoothly and requires less energy to go faster and farther when the wheels are in perfect alignment, you perform better when your thoughts, feelings, emotions, goals, and values are in balance."

Brian Tracy

Fractional Work

For many, the work that we really love falls into a very narrow band.

So narrow that the only way to do that and nothing else is to work for a very very large business. And many of us just aren't suited to surviving in really large companies. In fact, if the work that really lights you up is extremely specialised, it is probably not even possible to make a full-time job doing just that in any company, no matter how large.

Traditional work's answer to that is to give you some similar work to do as well. If you are lucky, this "filler" work is stuff that you can at least manage to do with good heart. Though more often than not, the makeweight work is stuff you really don't enjoy at all. It might even be stuff you hate – but you have to do it, don't you, to fill up your time.

Increasingly, companies are turning to fractional working to get specialist work done. I would love to say they do that so that workers don't have to do boring or undesirable (to them) filler tasks. In reality, it is more a case of companies realising that they are better off paying a little bit higher hourly rate for a shorter time for a real specialist in a task. They get a far better result, and don't need to pay the specialist rate for mundane tasks that a junior could do. The result of that, of course, is to leave our specialist with only a part-time job – hardly ideal for them!

This is where you can take advantage of the situation. If any one employer only needs a part of your time (the part spent doing what you love), that means you have a part of your time available to do other stuff. If you are lucky enough not to need a full-time salary, you can take that time and improve your life-work balance. Of course, if you *really* love the specialist work you do, your work-life balance is already sorted – it is all enjoyable stuff.

If however, like most, a full-time salary is actually necessary, you can go and do your specialist work for somebody else, to make up your full-time hours. And remember I said earlier that companies may well be prepared to pay an enhanced hourly rate for specialist work? It is entirely possible that the rate you now get paid by each of your employers is higher than you were on before – so your full-time hours are paying more in total!

Fractional working can even be a way to begin your move out of a full-time position and into a consultancy or portfolio career. I know many people who have combined a regular part-time PAYE position (fractional) with consultancy projects – which, of course, pay even better than regular specialist work.

For example, one manager worked out that roughly half of his time was spent on work that could easily be done by a junior, at half his salary. He suggested to his employer that he would continue to do the specialist work – the work he loved – for ten days a month. And the rest of his salary was used to employ a full-time junior, who not only did all the mundane work the manager used to do, she still had about 25% of her time spare to do other clerical work that needed doing. Meanwhile, the manager took on consultancy work in his specialist field, and more than made up the reduction in his salary. And got to spend 100% of his time on work he enjoyed.

There is an additional benefit for fractional workers too – they are more financially secure. As I write this, many economies around the world are seeing a lot of layoffs and redundancies. It probably won't be the last time we see that happen. If you have a full-time job and your employer has to let you go, you lose your entire income. But if you had been doing fractional work, you would only lose a part of your income.

Of course, fractional working won't work for every job, it is mainly appropriate for those that require specialist knowledge or experience. And if that is the part of your work that you truly love, there may be a way to make fractional working work for you.

Exercises

What parts of your work could be done by somebody less experienced than you?

Where else could you do the same work (non-competitive)?

Who would resist you doing your work on a fractional basis? Are they right?

When would fractional working be right for you and for the business?

How could you overcome the obstacles to fractional working? Would you want to?

Goals

Goal-setting is one of the least understood aspects of loving your work.

There is nothing less enjoyable than recording all those goals you missed

I am not saying you shouldn't have goals - of course you need to set yourself objectives – any fool can just bumble along with no particular aim in mind, and say they're loving their work. After all, who wouldn't enjoy doing work that it is impossible to fail at? Well, most people actually – while it might be pleasurable for a while to have such undemanding work, it would pretty soon become very dull.

So, if missing goals makes for unenjoyable work, and not having goals is boring, how can you use goals to help you love your work? Simply by making sure that the goals you set are both stretching and achievable – they challenge you, and they are within your capabilities. They also need to be capable of being met reasonably quickly.

That's not to say that you can't set yourself some long-term life or career goals, just that you also need to have some goals that create current challenge, and a way to know when that challenge has been met. Mihaly Csikszent-mihalyi, in his seminal work 'Flow: the psychology of optimal experience'[1] describes how even repetitive tasks can be made more enjoyable by the addition of simple goals and measures.

I put those principles to work when I took on some work for a seminar company. Part of the job was to call people who had signed up to attend a free event and check that they were going to turn up. Now, I don't enjoy calling strangers on the phone, so I wasn't exactly excited by this exercise. So each hour I gave myself the goal of making more calls and getting more "yes" responses than the previous hour. And I quickly found myself cheerfully making those last few calls, to achieve my small goal.

It is very important to acknowledge it when you achieve your interim goals, and to celebrate their achievement. Each one that you hit will give you a boost, and will strengthen your own internal belief that you are the sort of person who gets things done, a winner. So it is important that you take a brief pause to appreciate what you have achieved whenever you complete a goal.

The big mistake that people often make when setting goals, especially people who are working at their life's purpose, is to set an enormous end-goal, forgetting to build in smaller short-term goals along the way. The problem with that is not having a few small 'wins' that you can celebrate along the way can damage motivation and cause discouragement.

If the distance between the current state and the goal is too large, even great short-term results could still look like not making much progress, because the distance hasn't closed much. Imagine if the cyclists on the Tour de France didn't have stages and overnight results – the first day's riding, no matter how good, wouldn't get them much closer to their objective compared to the distance they still have to go.

So provide yourself with that all-important reminder of the progress you are making, that good feeling that comes with what Earl Nightingale, in "The Strangest Secret", called 'the progressive achievement of a worthy objective'. Set yourself some 'milestone' goals, and reward yourself for hitting them, along the way to your big life goal.

Exercises

What short, medium and long-term goals do you have for yourself?

Where will you be when you have achieved all your goals?

Whose help do you need to enlist to help you achieve your goals?

When do you review your progress against your written goals?

How does your current work contribute to your personal goals?

Higher Purpose

Many people wrongly think that they will be happy in their work if they can just get paid a bit more.

In my experience, and from what clients and colleagues tell me, that is rarely the case. The whole point of my mission to help you to do what you love for a living is that it is something that you would do even if you weren't getting paid at all – so surely it cannot be directly linked to how much you get paid to do it.

Where people have most success in turning what they love into a living, is where they are doing it for some higher purpose, something bigger than themselves. That can range from all-encompassing goals like ending hunger or creating world peace, to projects that just affect your local community or your spiritual group, your church, synagogue, temple or mosque. Or it may be as simple and powerful as just wanting your family to have everything they need.

Quite why this greater purpose makes people better at sticking at it until they can make a living doing what they love is open to debate, but I have my own theories.

Most of us have been brought up to think of work as something to be endured, something you do under duress, something done out of some kind of duty. So to spend your working life doing something you actually love seems kind of cheeky, something to be a bit guilty about. After all, who do we think we are, having fun in our work for goodness sake!

And that slight feeling of guilt makes us just a little bit less certain of our decision to create a work we can love. In turn, that uncertainty makes us less prepared to fight for our inalienable right to pursue happiness in our work. Somehow, telling the children that they can't have the latest designer trainers because Daddy or Mummy wants to *have fun* in the half their waking hours they are at work is not acceptable in the modern world.

But when you have a higher purpose, it's no longer just about having fun, it's also about your family's future, your spiritual beliefs, it's even all about saving the world! And now you are proud to stand up and stand out and say, "I love my work".

Just don't forget, you have to love the work itself. A chore being done for a grand purpose is still a chore, and will not be done with joy if the task itself is not something you can love. And you will never do something as well as someone who loves to do it, so you might even end up short-changing your worthy ideal. So by all means have a higher purpose that makes your work even more fulfilling – and serve that purpose doing work you love.

Exercises

What is your Higher Purpose?

Where in your work does your Higher Purpose show up?

Who are the people your Higher Purpose helps?

When do you feel most engaged with your Higher Purpose at work?

How does your Higher Purpose make you even better at your work?

H

© Thierry Maffeis – Fotolia.com

Many people worry so much about managing their careers, but rarely spend half that much energy managing their LIVES. I want to make my life, not just my job, the best it can be. The rest will work itself out.

Reese Witherspoon

Intuition, Inspiration & Intellect

As well as having a higher purpose, it helps if the actual work is something that gives your heart a lift.

This is where intuition and inspiration come in. They are how your heart and spirit find expression in your work. So as you achieve each task, you get a boost to your spirit, adding to your motivation and to your joy in your work.

Although in many ways they are similar, there is a fundamental difference between intuition and inspiration. Intuition is that little voice in the back of your head, that vague sense in your mind, that feeling in your gut, that an idea is something that could be good for you to do.

Inspiration, on the other hand, is that clear feeling that there is something you have to do, and this is it. You can ignore intuition without harming your spirit. You might harm your career, or your business, and end up doing something that's less than perfect, so it is not recommended, but you can do it. You ignore your inspiration at your peril.

Inspiration provides the energy, the impetus to do something brilliant. And intuition provides the check, the certainty that it is something that is really right for you, and you for it.

I'm often told that my methods are too analytical, that it is important to "just go with your gut". I would agree with that – you should absolutely listen to your gut, and your heart, and your spirit. My work focuses on finding the point at which inspiration and intuition meet intellect, those opportunities and activities that you can both enjoy and make a living doing.

I see far too many people making their decisions purely on the basis of logic, of "the numbers" stacking up, ignoring that little voice that is saying "this isn't for you". And then ending up miserable, but with a "good" job or business.

So should you just go with your heart, your inspiration? I would say probably not – you also need to check in with your gut, your intuition, to make sure it looks, sounds and feels right for you.

And also with your head, your intellect, to check that your dream job or business will actually succeed, that you really can make a living doing that work you love.

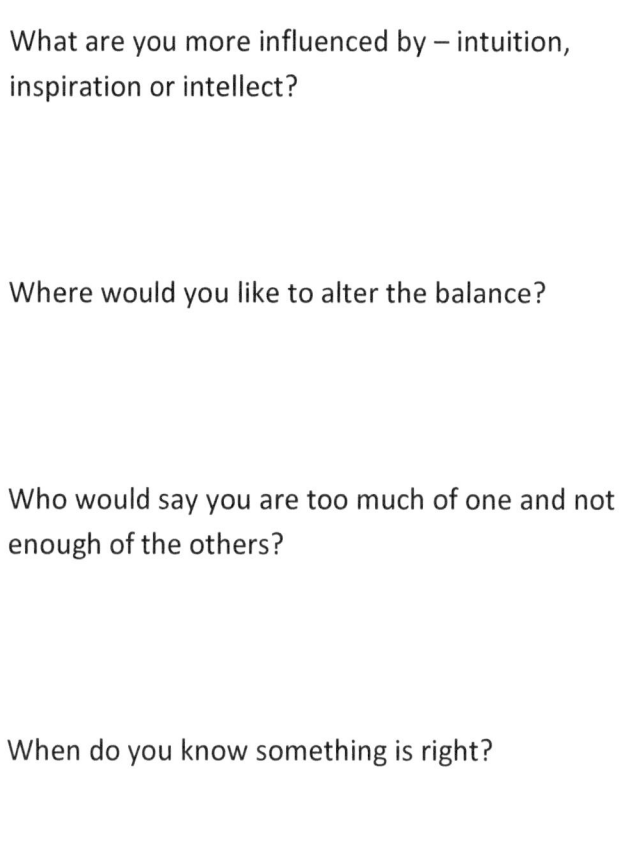

Exercises

What are you more influenced by – intuition, inspiration or intellect?

Where would you like to alter the balance?

Who would say you are too much of one and not enough of the others?

When do you know something is right?

How can getting the balance right make your work better?

One machine can do the work of fifty ordinary men.
No machine can do the work of one extraordinary man.

Elbert Hubbard

J.O.B.

There is a frightening phrase you will hear all over the personal and wealth development field: "J.O.B. = Just Over Broke"

What is meant by that is that you will never become wealthy working for someone else. In some respects, it is true - if all you are doing is holding down a steady job and somehow hoping that the pension will look after you when you are too old to swap time for money, then you could be setting yourself up for a pretty lean retirement.

Nonetheless, I think the 'Just Over Broke' concept is one of the most dangerous out there, because it turns a job into a kind of dirty word. And I can tell you from experience, leaping out of paid employment before you are properly prepared is a very good way to end up completely broke!

With my clients, I prefer to describe the J.O.B. as a "Judicious Opportunity to Breathe" - to take time to identify and refine their offer, and build up some reserves for their start-up period. When it is being done to fund a dream, even the most annoying of jobs becomes tolerable in the short term.

In any case, for many people a job is what best suits their temperament (but see also "F" for 'fractional working' for a potentially viable alternative). Many people love some elements of their job, and certainly love the freedom from financial worry it provides. And they also love the finance for training and investment it brings. There may be some elements of it that they would change - the boss, some of their colleagues - but on the whole they are happy with how they spend their workdays.

The right answer for them is not to throw in the job because of some self-help fallacy. It is to understand how they can become properly rewarded for what they love, within the context of an employment contract. And then, how to invest the proceeds effectively. While it is quite true that very few people achieve financial freedom from a job alone, there are loads who use their salary to fund the investments that will give them that freedom in the fullness of time.

Remember that going self-employed or starting your own business could mean the banks and mortgage lenders will view you as a poor credit risk, during your start-up period at least. That could mean you miss out on some investment opportunities, especially in property, because you cannot raise the finance. That is particularly relevant in a 'down' market such as we have as I write this, with lots of great property deals about but very little finance if your credit is anything other than excellent.

Before making the leap out of your job, or rushing to drop work that you are not enjoying, take time to understand the impact of doing that. Not just on your finances, but also on your lifestyle. Having less money (as will probably happen to start with) could mean that other parts of your life, things that add significantly to your personal fulfilment, are no longer possible.

Will you still be able to go out for nice meals, for example, or maybe the exotic travel will have to be cut back? Will you still be able to contribute to your favourite charity? What activities will your children not be able to take part in? And those expensive designer clothes you've been used to, will you have to think twice about those?

And think about your preferred working style. Would you just love to be able to make decisions without having to check with someone else, or do you prefer to have other people around to talk things through with. Do you work best in peace and quiet, or do you enjoy the chit-chat around the office, and those 'water-cooler' interactions? How would you deal with the isolation of working all on your own?

The simple fact is that not everybody is really cut out to be an entrepreneur, and it can be miserable to be out on your own struggling to get a business going. Some people just don't have the appetite for risk and tolerance of uncertainty that chucking in your job involves.

So, unless it is something you truly hate doing, the J.O.B. can be a great way to bank some cash to finance an eventual - and planned - move into your dream life.

J

Exercises

What do you think about your work?

Where do you see yourself on retirement?

Who do you need to think about when deciding on work style?

When could you consider a change in the way you work?

How would a job be right for you, rather than a business?

Kindness

Our attitude can be a major part of how much we enjoy our working environment.

I remember once being told about a talk by Zig Ziglar, the great guru of sales training, where he described a woman who came up to him after a seminar, asking for his help in getting out of a job where she said her colleagues were all unpleasant, negative people.

Zig's advice to her was to make a point of appreciating all the good things about her colleagues, to stop complaining about all their negative aspects, and to treat them all with kindness and respect. After much resistance, the woman went off and did as Zig suggested – and the next time they met, she reported how much her colleagues' attitudes had improved!

If you want to love your work, you need to have people around you who you enjoy being with. One of the great things about kindness is how infectious it is. When you take time to really appreciate the people around you, in no time at all they will start to appreciate you back. Of course, the same thing applies to all the negative emotions like jealousy, resentment and fear – people you are suspicious or fearful about will quickly start to be very nervous around you. So to enjoy going to work, a great start is to be kind to all your colleagues - keeping your attitude positive and full of real kindness.

I don't mean you have to become a doormat for them, or allow them to take out their foul moods on you. Just remain aware of all their good points, even when they are behaving badly, and remember that their grumpiness or unpleasantness probably has nothing whatever to do with you. My grandfather had a great saying, after dealing with someone in a bad mood – "Perhaps his feet hurt" he'd say in that kindly voice only grandfathers can manage.

And it is not just your relationship with colleagues you could improve with deliberate kindness. You could also make things better with your boss, and with the business as a whole, by setting out to be kind to them.

In his excellent book "The Magic of Thinking Big" David Schwartz writes about 'making yourself easier to lift'. What he means by that is that if you treat your boss well, go out of your way to make their job easier, put yourself out to help them achieve their objectives, then they are far more likely to help you move forward in your career. It was when I read David's words that I began to treat my then boss with kindness – and my career soon took a turn for the better.

Reaching kindness out beyond the organisation works too. In fact, it was a fundamental part of what I did in corporate life, Key Account Management. Where some account managers and sales directors would take great delight in putting one over on a client to grab a couple of extra points profit, the best always had a clear objective to really understand their contacts' needs, and then help them to meet them. Twice in my account management career I forgot that, and both times I lost big chunks of business, and also a job opportunity, several years later, because they had heard what I had done.

The whole point of customer service is to be kind to the company's clients, to leave them feeling significant and loved. How often have you been told by your friends and acquaintances about the salesperson or customer service agent who 'went the extra mile' for them, and left them feeling great about the company?

If you think about it, those staff who gave extra service not only saved themselves from a grumpy interaction with the customer, they also got themselves a wonderful shower of appreciation. A great way to get joy from your work!

One thing to bear in mind, though, if you use kindness to create an environment in which you can love your work: it only really works in the long term when it is authentic. People tend to see straight through it if you are only being nice to get what you want – if you really want to love your work, do it with genuine kindness to everyone you deal with.

Exercises

What is the level of kindness in your workplace?

Where in your work do you have the best opportunities to be kind?

Who would most benefit from some more kindness?

When do you feel least, and most, appreciated in your work?

How would more kindness enhance your working life?

L

Life-Work Balance

Of course, if you love your work, the whole concept of life-work balance flies out of the window. When what you do for a living is what you love to do anyway, all of your time is just life.

I remember once being told that somebody had asked Russian billionaire Roman Abramovich how many hours a day he worked. Puzzled, he thought for a bit, and then said none of what he spent his day doing felt like work to him. I can identify with that feeling – these days, there is not much that I do that feels like a chore.

But I don't think the work/life balance question goes away completely just because you are having fun at your work. It is still important to set aside time for family and friends, for loved ones, and for yourself. All work and no play, as the saying goes, makes Jack a dull boy (remember the film, The Shining?).

When you look carefully at that saying, you realise that 'dull' has a double meaning – dull, as in uninteresting, and dull, as in blunt. By concentrating excessively on just the business or career aspect of your life, you can actually become less good at your work, because you become one-dimensional. Creating space for a richer variety of inputs is essential.

Once when I was working as an account manager, I got involved in a project to improve our service to our biggest customers and to make a 'Customer Service Promise'. This involved completely reconstructing our inventory planning system, integrating it with an improved forecasting application. I was absolutely in my element, analysing and understanding our customers' requirements, and creating a system to deliver them. And that's all I did, for months – late into the evening, at weekends, whatever was needed. Eventually my boss took me to one side, and told me that I was getting really boring, because I had nothing else to talk about!

So make the time to go to the park with the family, or to take your partner out for a nice meal or to the theatre. Or to spend quality time with them in some other way. And allow yourself time to pursue a hobby - a hobby other than your work, that is!

Set aside time for your own development too, like reading inspiring books or meditating. And also create space in your life for maintaining your health – you could even combine that with family time by taking them swimming or for a walk.

If you are lucky enough – like me – to be able to follow your passion in the context of your own business or of a portfolio career, you will find that you have much greater flexibility in when you make time for family, friends and self.

The down-side to that ability is that if you are not careful that very flexibility will lead you to be working every hour there is – which will not go down at all well with even a highly supportive family.

Trust me, I know!

Exercises

What stops you getting the life/work balance right?

Where could you spend more time on one or the other?

Who would benefit most from an improved balance?

When do you find it hardest to maintain the balance?

How could you change how you work to come back into balance?

Mastery

Functional Knowledge (Hi/Lo) vs Industry / Company Knowledge (Lo/Hi)

Subject Master	Trusted Advisor
Commodity Contractor	Sector Expert

"Jack of All Trades and Master of None" is often used in a negative sense, implying that being a "Jack" at something is not enough.

In the old craft guilds, a 'Jack' was the term for a journeyman, someone who had completed their apprenticeship, someone competent but still honing their craft. And a great many journeymen made a decent living performing the craft they loved without ever becoming a master.

These days, we see a lot of generalists who know enough to be competent in a variety of areas, and who simply choose not to specialise. As consultants, they can make a decent living advising their clients on a variety of topics; as employees, they can rise through the business by knowing enough to know when they need to bring in outside expertise.

These broad-spectrum "Jacks" of business really can make a significant contribution to a company's success. According to a high-powered mergers and acquisitions expert I know, top quality true generalists are very rare, and so are very valuable.

The danger for generalists is that there are plenty of other "Jacks' with their level of functional knowledge, so they risk becoming what I call "commodity contractors" (see the matrix above). Because they have a lot of competitors, they quickly find themselves not being valued, and competing purely on price, just like a commodity product in the supermarket. So they find it hard to derive satisfaction or enjoyment in their work.

Where generalists start to come into their own is when they specialise in one particular industry, or even one company or organisation. Rather than being masters at a particular job, they become experts in a sector. They know the business so well, and some functions well enough, that they add more value than would a subject master in those functions. Their specific industry knowledge is also a form of mastery.

Where the most value – and enjoyment in work – lies is in specialising on both functional and sector lines. When a subject master is also an expert in a sector, they can become a true trusted advisor. Their superlative functional work coupled with their expertise in the sector means that their clients and employers trust them to bring in other subject masters for the areas they are not best at. And that allows them to do only the work they truly love, and to surround themselves with a team they enjoy working with.

Exercises

What level are you at now, Jack or Master?

Where on the matrix do you see yourself?

Who would support you to become more of a Master?

When you look at the matrix, where would you like to be?

How can you go about positioning yourself there?

"The secret of life is to have a task, something you devote your entire life to, something you bring everything to, every minute of the day for the rest of your life."

Henry Moore

"No": learn how to say it

One of the best ways to lose your love of work is to agree to things that don't excite you, that leave you feeling bored or hassled.

You know the sort of thing, that new project your favourite client gave you, because "I know it's not what you normally do, but I know I can trust you to do a good job of it". And it then takes you twice as long to do as it should have, for two different, but related, reasons. Firstly, you don't have all the answers readily to hand (after all, it is outside of your usual work). And second, you keep putting it off, because you know from the start it is not something you are going to enjoy.

And it is even worse if you are in a job, and it is your boss who has placed such trust in you that they have kindly given you "the opportunity to expand your experience". In that situation, chances are you will still be expected to carry on doing all the tasks you normally do - things which, if you have worked to get into a position of loving your work, are things you actually enjoy. Plus the new task, that you are not going to enjoy, expansion opportunity or not. So overwhelm rears its ugly head, a great way to stop you enjoying even the work you love.

So how do you cope with those kinds of demands? Just say "No"? Well, that's one option – though not one that is going to endear you to your boss or your favourite client. A far better solution is to make sure that your network includes colleagues and collaborators who are great at, and enjoy, the kind of work that sits either side of yours, the sort of stretch of your normal remit I just described. Then, when a client asks "Will you do this for me?" you can respond by saying that, much as you would love to, they'd be far better off using Joe, who is an absolute Master at this stuff, and for whom you can personally vouch.

That may be harder to pull off when you are in a job and it is your boss asking – but if your internal network is strong you should be able to think of somebody who would do a better job than you. And don't be afraid to suggest an external consultant – unless you are genuinely under-worked, your boss will be well aware of the risk that your existing work may suffer, and could welcome a cost-effective solution that doesn't adversely impact your job performance.

And if they don't, at least you have highlighted the risk, and let them know that this isn't work you would take on by choice. In my experience, very few employers actively set out to make their team unhappy, but if they don't know, they can't do something about it.

If someone insists on you doing something they know you won't enjoy and won't do well, it may be time to find some other work. But if you have not said "No" to the work you are not going to enjoy, I can pretty much guarantee that you will end up resenting it, and them for 'making you do it'. That is rather unfair, if you didn't let them know you would rather not do it.

The resentment is actually aimed at yourself, because deep down you know you didn't do anything to avoid that work, but we humans are generally not very good at taking responsibility, so you look outside for someone to blame.

So be fair to yourself and to everyone else, and when you really don't want to do work you won't enjoy, be prepared to say so.

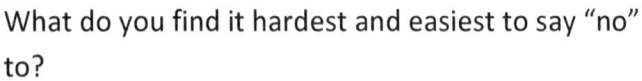

Exercises

What do you find it hardest and easiest to say "no" to?

Where would you draw the line?

Who in your network could you pass work on to?

When can you reasonably say "no" and when can't you?

How can you make it easier to say "no"?

Opportunities

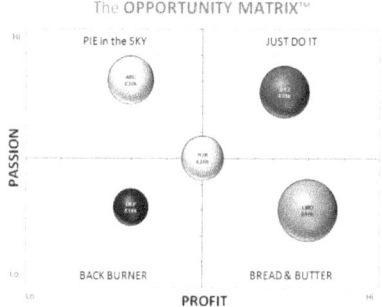

The OPPORTUNITY MATRIX™

Making a living doing what you love means picking opportunities to say "Yes" to.

The opportunities need to satisfy just two major criteria: that they involve you doing work that you will love, and that you can make a living doing them. Or at the very least that they'll make a contribution to your success that is balanced with the amount of time, money, effort and resources that you commit to them.

In other words, they have to answer the two "Big Business Questions":

How much do you want to do this?

Will you make any money at it?

I use a deceptively-simple four-box matrix to decide which opportunities to focus on. On the vertical axis is "Passion", or how much you'll love doing them. And on the Horizontal axis is "Profit", will you be able to make a living from them.

The ones you want are the ones that score high on both – you really want to do them AND you can make decent money at them (or whatever more holistic measure you choose). I call those "Just Do It" opportunities.

Most people have at least one opportunity in the quadrant I call "Pie in the Sky" – lots of passion and very little profit. Others, often the same people, have opportunities in what I call the "Bread and Butter" quadrant – dead easy to make a living at, in fact you're probably already doing it, and it bores you to tears.

The good news is that there's a solution to this dichotomy: stick with the "Bread & Butter", for now, and use the money from that to fund the development of the "Pie in the Sky" projects so that they become more viable – moving them across into the "Just Do It" box. Some people like to call that "going to the cash machine".

And here's something really strange: as soon as the boring, annoying, irritating "Bread & Butter" work is no longer forever, you'll remember what it was about it that you used to enjoy. And it will also start to shift towards "Just Do It"! At this point, I will warn that you got bored with it once, and you'll probably get bored with it again, so best to focus on moving the Passion Project from "Pie in the Sky" to "Just Do It".

So what do you do if you don't have anything that scores high on "Profit"? There is no easy answer here – you will have to go back to the drawing board. You might need to redefine what represents a healthy level of income, maybe you are setting your sights unrealistically high (see G for Goals). Or you may need to include some options that you have previously discounted, maybe on the grounds that you don't want to do them. Remember what I said under J for "J.O.B." – sometimes we need to be pragmatic and find ways to enjoy work we wouldn't choose, for a while, while we plan our dream work. Getting to a position of loving your work isn't something you can just switch on, it will take some effort – so that you don't have to work for ever.

Exercises

What opportunities do you or your business have right now?

When do you find it hard to decide what to say "yes" to?

Where on the Opportunity Matrix are your opportunities?

Who should sanity-check your assessment?

How else could you assess your opportunities?

Pay

If you are going to make a living doing what you love, you're going to need to be paid. Otherwise it's just a hobby.

Maybe one you absolutely adore, but a hobby nonetheless. My friend and guide Nick Williams, who runs the Inspired Entrepreneur community, always says there's a difference between working for pay, and getting paid to work. He says working for pay is, literally, just that – the pay is the only reason for the work; if you were not getting paid for it, you simply wouldn't do it. All you are doing when you work for pay is swapping time (and energy, and spirit) for money.

Sometimes in life, we have to swap our time for the money we need to pay our bills. The trick is not to get sucked into the idea that getting money is enough, that so long as we work hard and get enough pay, everything will be alright. I can tell you from painful experience, that's a good way to damage both your physical and mental health, if you can't find a way to enjoy the work you are doing for pay.

Getting paid to work is a different proposition altogether: the reason for doing the work is because it's your passion, your purpose, your mission. Not the money. The money is what is going to allow you to carry on with the work – what Nick calls 'the work you were born to do'. It is what makes it possible for you to continue to bring your special skills and talents to the world. It is what will allow you to lead a fulfilled and happy life.

Singer-songwriter Leonard Cohen sums it up well, in something he said when talking about his motivations when he set out on his career:

"I didn't want to work for pay, but I wanted to be paid for my work."

A rather bizarre quirk of human nature (in most people, anyway) is that we seem to feel a need to have made some kind of sacrifice in exchange for payment. We seem to have an issue with getting paid for something that came easy and that we enjoyed. If our wealth or reward doesn't come from sacrifice or suffering, it feels somehow immoral or unethical. But how daft is that?

We have it completely backward. The time when we are contributing the most - to our employers, to our clients, to the world – is precisely when we are doing what comes naturally to us, that is effortless, that is a joyful experience.

So it makes sense that it should also be what we get paid the most for – highest value, highest pay!

Exercises

What is the reason for your work, Pay or Passion?

Where would you work if money wasn't a factor?

Who would you work for if you had completely free choice?

When would you stop work if you didn't need the money?

How can you get paid to do work you love? (assuming you don't already!)

"Where your talents and the needs of the world cross, therein lies your vocation."

Aristotle

Questions: ask better ones

There are only two big questions that need to be answered about our work:

How much do I want to do this?

Will I make any money at it?

Everything else is detail. It's only after we can give a positive answer to those two fundamental questions that we need to get into the nitty-gritty of business plans and job definitions, and goals, objectives and targets.

All too often, I come across people who are using precious time trying to understand the finer points of a task that obviously fails to satisfy the first fundamental test. They drive themselves (and others) mad with loads of 'what-if' questions, when the whole thing is pointless because they are never going to enjoy the work enough to be great at it anyway.

So does that mean that if what you are passionate about won't pay well enough, you should give up on doing it for a living? No, not at all. That's why this section talks about asking better questions.

If the work passes the first test (can you love it) but falters at the second (will it pay enough), idly wishing for ways to make it pay just isn't going to cut it. Nor are questions about why it won't pay well enough. The better question is not

"Why won't I be able to make enough doing what I love?", but "HOW could I get paid enough for this work?"

Your unconscious mind is very obedient when helping you to answer queries. When you ask yourself "why can't I ...?", your unconscious mind merrily seeks out all the things that confirm the presupposition in that question – which is, that you cannot. And when you ask yourself "how could I ...?", then your unconscious dutifully delivers all the ways that satisfy the positive presupposition inherent in that question – that you *can*.

So if you want to make a living doing what you love, make sure your questions all presuppose that ... you really can!

There's another trick to use in the questions you ask, which also fools your unconscious mind into taking a positive approach. Wherever possible, add the words "even more" to your questions. For example: "How can I make even more money doing what I love?" The presup-position in this question is that you are already making some money, and your unconscious mind will think "Oh, OK, we're already making some money, great, then it can't be all that hard to make some more!"

Your conscious mind can be fully aware that you are not yet making money doing what you love, but that doesn't matter. Your unconscious will accept the presupposition, that's the way it works. Of course, if you really are already making some money doing what you love, that's even better.

A warning here, the unconscious does not know how to process a negative. So don't ask it questions like "How can I do less of the work I hate?" – all it will hear is "how" and "do the work I hate", and it will dutifully find ways to keep doing the thing the question is focused on. So turn it around, and focus on what you want instead – that might be "How can I do more of the work I love?" or it might be "How can I have more leisure time?"

You will need the willing support of your unconscious mind to work out how to make a living doing work you love, so make sure all your questions feed it positive presuppositions.

Exercises

What are your answers to the two big questions?

Where might your career or business fail the big questions?

Who do you need to involve to get or maintain positive answers to them?

When do you find yourself asking questions that focus on the negative?

How could you make your questions even more positive? *(did you see what I did there ☺)*

Resentment: avoid it

One of the best ways *not* to love your work is to spend time worrying about what people have done to you.

What if XYZ Co hadn't turned me down for that job? What if my boss hadn't given me that impossible deadline to meet? What if a colleague I helped out hadn't taken all the credit & got the promotion I wanted? What if ... ? What if you just focused on the future, instead of on the past? What if you focused on what those experiences taught you, instead of the supposed harm they did you? Wouldn't that be a better question?

That is not to say I agree with the concept of "No regrets". Though I guess it depends what you understand by "regret". I define it as wishing you hadn't done something, or had done something differently. So it does seem rather foolish not to regret some of the stuff I have done in the past – coasting my way to a third class degree, thinking I could get past the muppet turning right against my motorcycle, taking *that* job ... the list is endless!

Did I learn stuff from those mistakes? Absolutely! Which is why I now wish I hadn't done them – i.e. I regret them. Refusing to regret things that you've done implies refusing to get the learnings from them.

But there is a big difference between regretting stuff you did (or didn't do for that matter) and feeling bad about stuff that others did that harmed or hurt you. I rather wish that certain people had treated me differently. It would have been nice if certain bosses had recognised my enormous talents. And it sure would have helped if the muppet in that Citroen hadn't decided to turn across my path that damp December night.

But I cannot regret any of that – you can only regret your own actions. The equivalent to regret when it concerns other people's actions is resentment. That doesn't help you grow like all the learning experiences you quite reasonably regret, it eats you up by placing the cause of your success or failure outside of yourself.

For years I blamed my bosses or my clients for things not going right. I excused myself from my responsibility by making their unreasonable behaviour to blame for what went wrong. And sometimes they really did behave unbelievably badly toward me.

I held that resentment close to my heart, always on the lookout for the next idiot who was going to do me down. And yes, along they came, same old situation, all over again. It took me a very long time to work out that the one constant in all my unsatisfactory work relationships was … me!

The biggest danger of all is if you start to beat yourself up about the things you did to yourself, the things you regret. You did them, you can't change that, and holding it against yourself instead of learning from it is just plain silly. That serves no purpose – it doesn't even make you feel better temporarily, like holding grudges against other people can. If resentment against others poisons your heart, then resentment against yourself is corrosive to your very soul.

So yes, I regret loads of stuff – and I resent nothing.

Exercises

What regrets do you have?

Where in your career have you felt resentment?

Who have you resented, either as a boss, a client or a colleague?

When has resentment made you feel better about yourself?

How could you have a more positive feeling?

Self-Awareness

It may seem obvious, but it is worth saying that actually knowing yourself, knowing what matters to you, and knowing how you tick is an essential part of loving your work.

When you understand what sort of person you are, what you handle well and what you prefer not to have to deal with, then it is far easier to relax into the right sort of work – for you.

Apart from deep introspection (which has its place – one of my favourite self-awareness tools, Core Process, is a guided introspective exercise), the best way to understand yourself is through profiling systems. These are often, mistakenly, all called psychometric tests – in fact some are personality-based, some preference-based, and some behaviour-based. None of them give a complete picture, so I always recommend using a variety of them, depending on what you need to find out about yourself.

My personal favourites are Myers-Briggs Type Indicator (MBTI) for personality, Belbin's Team Roles, DISC behavioural profiling, and, for how you fit into entrepreneurial teams, Wealth Dynamics (see the Resources pages for more details of each of these). There are a vast number of others, these are just the ones I have used, and I find useful in the context of loving your work.

Something to be very cautious about when using a profiling system is the tendency to use the results to put yourself in a box and identify yourself as the profile: "I'm an ENTP", "I'm a Specialist", "I'm a Star". You are so much more than that!

The best way to use profiling systems to help you love your work, is to refer to them whenever you find yourself feeling uncomfortable or unmotivated by a task or a role. Identify those aspects of the activity that don't sit well with one of your profiles, and then look for ways to reduce or eliminate them. And conversely, when you find particular joy in something, compare it to your profiles to understand how it fits – and then you can find ways to do more of it.

Profiling is a great start to gaining self-awareness, particularly if you use the services of an expert to get both an accurate profile and a thorough understanding of how that relates to your personal individual situation. It's helpful to have somebody to reflect back to you what they see in how you approach your work. Somebody who can help you to spot when a particular task or situation leaves you 'flat' or on edge; and somebody who can highlight those things that really light you up. We often don't take time to notice when we're truly in our flow – we're too busy experiencing the joy of our work.

That is one of the core elements of what Csikszentmihalyi[1] defines as "Flow"– that you forget about everything except the experience. So having someone – a friend, a colleague, a coach – to point it out is critical. Even better, a number of different people, maybe a master-mind or peer support group, to get several perspectives. The important thing is that we accept their feedback with an open mind. We may conclude that they are mistaken, but the fact that they saw us this way could tell us something useful about how we interact with others.

Self-awareness doesn't always have to come from within!

Exercises

What profiling tools have you used?

Where in your career or business could more self-awareness help you?

Who knows you best and would give you honest feedback?

When are you truly in your flow?

How could you become even more self-aware?

Trust

There are three ways trust is important to loving your work: trust that colleagues, clients and bosses will treat you fairly, trust that others have in you, and trust that you have in yourself.

Trusting that others will treat you fairly is the most obvious way trust affects how much you can love your work. If you are constantly on your guard against people taking advantage of you, doing you down somehow, or generally not playing fair, then it will be incredibly hard to relax, find your flow and enjoy your work. Even if the tasks themselves are ones you would find joy in, if you feel that you have to watch out for yourself all the time, that wariness will wear you down and over time will over-ride the enjoyment.

Allied to that, having confidence that others believe you will do a great job makes it far easier to get into your flow doing the things that you love. You can focus on the joy of doing your work, without worrying about whether others are happy with how you are doing.

That feeling of being trusted makes an enormous difference to how much you can enjoy your work, because it gives you a feeling of being in control, of doing the work for its own sake, not for other people. Csikszentmihalyi[1] identifies this "auto-telic" nature of work – the work being the goal in itself

– as being a core component of the "Flow" experience of loving your work.

And that ability to make the work itself the important thing, to focus purely on the joy of doing the work you love, is made even easier when you are able to trust yourself to deliver a superb outcome for clients and employers. If you doubt your ability to provide sufficient value for others, it distracts you from your focus on the task, and the pleasure of it.

When you have that feeling deep inside, that freedom from proving yourself to anyone else, it makes for an easy, comfortable and relaxed enjoyment of the wonder and joy of the work you love.

Of course, trust cuts both ways. In exactly the same way that you want to experience those aspects of trust so that you can love your work, so do other people you work with. The first two, you can directly give to people, and how you behave with them will have a significant effect on the third.

Just as you need to trust that people will play fair with you, they need to trust that you will do the same with them. In fact, by playing fair yourself, you are increasing the likelihood of everyone else doing so. Similar to kindness, it only takes one individual to start to demonstrate trust to change the whole culture of a workplace. And it only takes one to display distrust to destroy it for everyone.

You can demonstrate your trust that others will perform their work competently and effectively, just as you want them to trust your competence. The best way to do that is to empower them to do it their own way, without trying to micromanage them, so long as they produce the required results.

And your trust in them to do the work well, and to behave in a trustworthy manner, will add to their ability to trust themselves and really get into the flow of their work. They have the same desire as you do, to love their work, and helping them to do that will make your own work even more joyful.

T

Exercises

What level of trust is there in your work environment?

Where would you like to see more trust?

Who could have more trust in whom?

When do you feel completely trusted?

How could you have more trust in your work?

Umbrella

When I speak about focus, I usually start with the mnemonic: "Follow One Course Until Successful"

Many people misinterpret that to mean sticking to just one activity, a tight niche, restricting them in what work they can do. For a lot of people, that would actively get in the way of loving their work – they need a certain amount of variety in their working week to allow them to feel fulfilled.

But that is not what Follow One Course Until Successful means – it is one general "course", not path, not track, not single line.

A course is a general umbrella under which everything you do fits. Speaker and presenter Katie Ledger describes it as "a single red thread that runs through everything you do". By understanding what your umbrella or "red thread" is, you can quickly and easily decide whether something you have the opportunity to do will be something you actually want to do.

So how do you decide what your 'umbrella' should be? Take some time to think about what is truly important to you, and what activities make you feel that you have had a really great and productive day. Those two aspects will give the framework of your umbrella. The things that are important to you – your values – will be the shaft, that holds everything together. And the things that you have a talent for, the things that you enjoy and do well, will be the ribs, extending out from the shaft.

Now you need to come up with an overall description, the all-encompassing fabric of your umbrella, that holds it all together as a single whole, one that you and other people can understand. That way, you can select the things that fall within your umbrella, and you can let your bosses and clients know what work to ask you to do for them.

Without a clear vision of your 'value umbrella' under which fit all the ways you serve people, whether that's employers, customers or clients, you will find it harder to choose the work that will bring you true satisfaction. And if you don't have clear guidelines for yourself and others of what work you want to be doing, you will end up doing work that just doesn't light you up.

That would be a terrible waste of your unique talents, so understand what umbrella term or phrase you're going to use to describe your ideal work, make others aware of it, and spend your life doing work you truly love.

My 'umbrella' is making people happier and more effective by helping them to focus on their core opportunities and activities, that they love and that will produce their success. There are a number of ways I do that: For some clients I handle the commercial relationship with their key clients, so they can focus on the delivery of what they are really brilliant at. For others, I help them to identify their own 'umbrella', and how to stick to opportunities that fit within it.

And for some time I had a separate business, that saved independent consultants from worrying about their computers falling over. My technical partner in that business is a strange beast, he actually enjoys getting computers to behave themselves! But he's hopeless when it comes to systems and processes and things that I love, so we support each other to focus on the work we love to do. And the business fits under my umbrella because it frees our clients from PC hassles and allows them to focus on the things they do well, and love to do.

When you have a clearly-defined umbrella term, people will find it much easier to bring you the kind of work or the kind of opportunities that you are going to love.

Exercises

What name would you give your 'umbrella' or 'red thread'?

Where do you do work that is hard to include in your umbrella?

Who, apart from yourself, would most gain from knowing your umbrella?

When would knowing your umbrella focus be helpful to you ?

How will you check new work fits under your umbrella?

Value-Add

It is essential that you find a way for doing what you love to add value for others. You need them to be exchanging their hard-earned money for what you have to offer.

Or maybe not-so-hard earned, for them, if they've already got the hang of loving their work! The point is, that money is the best way we have (at the moment, anyway) of keeping score. I said under 'Pay' that the more value added, the higher the pay. A corollary of that is that the more money that people are going to pay for your work, the more value you will have had to provide to really earn that money. And the more value they will expect in exchange for it.

What's important is to remember that it is not you who places the value on what you provide. You get to set the price, but that is not the same as value. Value is determined by the buyer – Roman scholar Publilius Syrus famously said "*A thing is worth whatever a man is prepared to pay for it.*"

So don't make assumptions about your pricing – a classic mistake new entrepreneurs make is to assume that because their service is dead easy for them to provide, it has little value. For a creative designer to 'knock up' a quick page layout may seem too easy to be paid seriously for it; for a left-brain analytical type like me, it would take the best part of half a day – and still look rubbish!

So how much is that half-hour of a designer's time worth to me? Four hours plus – yet the likelihood is I will only be charged an hour. Which means there has been a creation of value – I have paid the designer for an hour of their time, and saved three hours of mine. And they have actually spent only half an hour on it. Net gain: three and a half hours!

And I got a better job done, into the bargain. The value of that could be far more than the time I saved – it could mean more clients or higher charges. Once I take that value into account, whatever their fee was, it will seem reasonable.

It's called the comparison frame – setting up the real value to the client, then comparing how little, in comparison, your fee will be. So my designers don't need to be too worried about charging me too much – so long as there is true value-add in the transaction.

And nor do you have to worry – always remember your joyful work is another's hell, your delight their despair, your passion their burden, so regardless of how much you love doing it, take your full reward for relieving them of it!

Exercises

What work do you love to do that others hate?

Where do you add the most value?

Who do you add value for?

When do people really value what you love to do?

How can you find more people to add more value for?

"Try not to become a man of success but rather try to become a man of value."

Albert Einstein

Win-Win (-Win)

Business is not a zero-sum game. It is not a case of grabbing your share of the pie, and the more you get, the less your client gets to keep. Just bake a bigger pie!

And the way to do that is to work together with clients or employers to add more ... value.

I remember arguing vehemently with my Sales Director once, about the prices a client was paying. They wanted to resell our products into a market that needed a particular solution inside a particular budget. At the current price, our product worked as a part of that solution; at the increased price I was being asked to get, it was going to be far too expensive.

If our client got the extra business, sales would go through the roof – the pie that we had to share between us would get bigger. A lot bigger. So our smaller <u>proportion</u> of the profit was still a very much bigger amount of money. A real win-win outcome – our client won more business, and so did we.

And it doesn't have to be all about price – you can create a bigger pie by doing things like training clients or colleagues so they can perform better and win more business, in turn making your business bigger. The important thing is to look for ways that you can both win.

It works in jobs too. If you want to earn more money, you can either demand a salary increase for carrying on as you are, or you can agree that you will get a share of increased profits that come as a result of doing something new.

It is best to get that agreed upfront, though, not wait until after it has happened. There are two reasons for that: firstly your boss is more likely to agree to sharing a non-existent (so far) larger pie, and secondly (and more importantly for you) a major factor in people loving their work is a clear link between effort and reward.

So, you have won, and your client or boss has won. And what about that third win? That's your client's (or your employer's) customer. The pie is not going to get bigger unless they are getting a better deal too, so they buy more of the product or service because it is a win for them too.

And the people they come into contact with win too, either because they have more spare cash to share, or because they are happier with their better deal. We could add any number of extra wins, really.

In a world that is governed not by jealously guarding our own little gain, but by working together to grow a bigger pie, everyone can win.

Exercises

What win-win-win interactions do you create?

Where does competition reduce your enjoyment of your work?

Who in your work just wants a bigger share of the existing pie?

When does hard-headed competition work?

How could you get more by creating a bigger pie?

"The reality today is that we are all interdependent and have to co-exist on this small planet. Therefore, the only sensible and intelligent way of resolving differences and clashes of interests, whether between individuals or nations, is through dialogue."

The Dalai Lama

eXperience

© Kurhan – Fotolia.com

OK, I know, it's a bit of a cheat - the alternative was to talk about enjoying all the "Xylophone" of tones of work – I don't think you want that?

Sometimes you don't have all the experience you need to make a living doing what you love.

In Enjoyment-Performance Theory (see "E"), we talked about how you enjoy what you do well, and you perform well at what you enjoy. That assumes a start-point of you having a certain level of ability, but that doesn't have to be the case.

If there is something that you feel you would enjoy doing for a living, but you don't yet do it well enough to make a living at it, there is nothing to stop you from setting out to gain experience in doing it. So, eventually becoming better at it, good enough to make a good living doing it.

In a job, you can ask for assignments or projects that give you the experience. Or you can ask for a transfer to another department where you can learn the new skill. It could mean taking a drop in salary for a while, so there is a risk involved, and it is important to be clear on what your long-term objective is.

And if you are in business, there is nothing wrong with taking lower-paid work that allows you to gain it, or even going back into a job for a while. Many successful people have done just that, taking low-paid jobs to understand a new area of business, before launching their own unique slant on it.

Success trainer Christopher Howard describes how he took a basic job with Dale Carnegie Training, in order to learn more about running a successful seminar business. Following his lead, I worked for his UK promoter for a while, following up on sales leads by phone, so that I could learn to be more effective on the telephone. And I helped out at Chris' UK events to learn about the issues involved in putting on a major personal development seminar.

There is also another aspect of experience that contributes to you loving your work: your ability to learn from it, and avoid repeating the same mistakes over again. Those might be mistakes that get you into trouble with bosses or clients, or they might be errors that frustrate your desire to deliver great value. They might be mis-steps on your career path that led you into work you didn't enjoy.

Whatever they are, so long as you learn from them, and use that knowledge to help you add even more value next time, then they are not a problem – in the long term, anyway. So make sure you are not one of those 'veterans', you know the sort, the guys who have been in and around business for decades, but they have just one year's experience – repeated many, many times!

The last part of experience as a factor in loving your work is requisite variety. Some of us just love a routine, and we are only able to relax if things won't suddenly change. Others get bored in a nanosecond, and need to be doing something different as often as possible.

Always remembering what I said in the introduction about focus, you need to organise your work life so that it provides just the right amount of new experiences for you to satisfy your natural curiosity without it overwhelming you.

So, gain experience of what you want to do, learn from your own experience, and make your work life a rich and varied experience.

Exercises

What experience would you like to add to your portfolio?

Where could you get that experience?

Who can help you get it, or introduce you to someone who can?

When have you had experiences that you have learned from? (You *did* learn, didn't you?)

How much variety is right for you, and how can you get more or less to suit you?

You-nique

There are something like seven billion people in the world. And you are just one.

That makes you rarer than the most precious of gems, more singular than the most iridescent of pearls, more unique than the finest work of art. So the last thing you want to be is just like every-body else![2]

Most of us have heard marketers speak about needing to identify our company's USP, its 'Unique Selling Point'. Writer and success guru Harv Eker takes the concept a bit further, and talks about each of us having what he calls our 'You-nique' Selling Point.

Because no two of us are the same, every single one of us is different in some subtle way from everyone else. And that is what makes employers and clients want to work with us, because they genuinely cannot get exactly what we offer anywhere else.

In Neuro-Linguistic Programming (NLP) there is a concept of "filters" through which you make meaning of the world. They are things like your culture, your upbringing, your individual experiences, each of which colours how you view the world. What that means is that you have a subtly, finely, marginally different view of the world from everybody else

– and that is what you get paid for, for your You-nique way of making sense of the world.

The importance of that for loving your work is that you really do not have to try to squeeze yourself into somebody else's box, their view of who you should be. Have you ever noticed that it is the outspoken people, the people who speak their mind, the ones who do their own thing, who tend to get on in their career, their business and their life?

One of the best account managers I ever worked with was also the most highly opinionated. And she wouldn't take any nonsense from anyone else in the business, no matter what their position. She would happily take on Executive Directors if she thought they were getting in the way of good client service. She is now a senior executive with a major consumer goods company, and, as always, is having a great time in her work.

Richard Branson's biggest value is that he is prepared to be different; in fact, that's the only reason he ever goes into an industry, because he can see how to do things better. Bill Gates dropped out of Harvard to pursue his different kind of computing. Oprah Winfrey uses her unique position to pursue her passion to improve people's lives. Each of them recognised that being different, being 'you-nique', is the best way to enjoy your work.

I am not suggesting that you should become a trouble-maker – the people who make the most difference are those who are able to be authentic in their work without making themselves a pain in the backside. They understand their uniqueness, and they understand that other people don't see the world as they do. They learn to translate their world for the people trying to 'stick to the rules'. And they understand that if they tried to conform, if they tried to act like somebody else, if they tried to make their world work through someone else's filters, they would end up doing a very bad job of it.

So instead of being just a pale imitation of somebody else, you can release your spirit, that you-nique essence of You, and make the difference you were always meant to make to your company, to your society and to your world.

Exercises

What is your You-niqueness based on?

Where do you stand out from the rest of the world?

Who are you most like, and most unlike, in how you do you work?

When do you most see things differently from others?

How are you uniquely qualified to do what you love to do better?

Zeal

Zeal, passion, enthusiasm ... no matter what you call it, if what you do for a living doesn't totally light you up with excitement every work-day morning, you haven't found the work you love.

I have left this most important aspect of loving your work until last, so if you remember nothing else, remember this. Far too many people drag themselves out of bed every Monday morning thinking 'Oh God, I've got to go to work today!'; when you're making a living doing the work you love, you leap out of bed on a Monday morning, shouting: 'Ooh good – I get to go to work today!"

That passion for what you do will shine through. If you have your own business, clients will sense it and find you a joy to work with. If you have a job, employers and colleagues will sense it ... and find you a joy to work with. Think about it – if you have to engage someone to do a task for you, who would you rather ask, someone who will do it grudgingly or someone who will do it joyfully?

And if you are asked to recommend someone to do some work, do you suggest someone who'll huff and puff and moan about it, someone who is doing it just to pay their bills? Or does your mind go straight to the person who will do it with a spring in their step and a song in their heart?

And don't forget Enjoyment-Performance Theory ("E") – if you are passionate about your work, you will perform it much better than someone who is doing it just for the money. You will be prepared to do that little extra, to go the extra mile to create a result you can be truly proud of. Employers and clients notice that - and they reward it, with promotions, referrals and contracts.

And your zeal for your work will lead you to tell them what you did extra, and why you did it. Not because you want them to see what a great worker you are (even though you are), but because your sheer passion and exuberance about your work will leave you wanting them to be as enthused as you are about how brilliantly it worked out.

People buy results and outcomes; but even more than that, they buy confidence – and confidence is conveyed more than anything else by your enthusiasm, your passion, your sheer *zeal* for the work you love.

Exercises

What part of your work do you get most excited about?

Where does your enthusiasm come from?

Who do you dampen your enthusiasm in front of? Why?

When do you feel most full of zeal about your work?

How could you enthuse yourself and others even more?

A	**Action**	stop procrastinating
B	**Busy Fool**	make your activity purposeful
C	**Clarity**	exactly what work you love to do
D	**Decisions**	research for good ones
E	**Enjoyment-Performance**	we do best what we enjoy
F	**Fractional Work**	several employers
G	**Goals**	little ones as well as big ones
H	**Higher Purpose**	a 'why' that is bigger than you
I	**Inspiration, Intuition, Intellect**	use all three
J	**J.O.B.**	not something to be ashamed of
K	**Kindness**	use it on everyone in your work
L	**Life-Work Balance**	don't be a dull boy or girl
M	**Mastery**	expert at something
N	**No**	when and how to say it
O	**Opportunities**	that you love AND make money
P	**Pay**	don't work for it, be paid to work
Q	**Questions**	possibility and even more
R	**Resentment**	don't do it (and do regret)
S	**Self-Knowledge**	knowing what you love to do
T	**Trust**	fairness, others and yourself
U	**Umbrella**	everything you do fits
V	**Value-Add**	why you get paid
W	**Win-Win-Win**	bake a bigger pie
X	**eXperience**	gain and learn from it
Y	**You-nique**	there is only one you
Z	**Zeal**	inspired and required

Summary

Doing what you love for a living needs a number of things to be in place, each of which is important. From practical issues like actually making a living, to your spiritual and emotional fulfilment, it all has to be present: focus and clarity, a higher purpose, adding value, control over your working life, mental and spiritual stimulation, and most of all you have to be enthusiastic about it.

If you are clear in your mind about what kind of work you enjoy, and you can explain simply and concisely what kind of work you want to focus on, then employers and clients can start to bring it to you. And focus will give you a framework to avoid becoming a busy fool, and to make the right decisions to keep you doing the work you love to do.

Loving your work is rarely about the money. There is nearly always some higher purpose that the money is for – ranging from providing for your own family, to making the world a better place for our global family. On aeroplanes, they say to fix your own oxygen mask first, before you try to help others; the same goes for your higher purpose – to make the difference you were born to make, you first need to make a living for yourself.

The way to make a living doing what you love is to find the way that your passion adds value for others. The more value you create, the better a living you will be able to make. It's not about making sure you grab your share, it's about working with others to create more value, to bake a bigger pie, so there is enough for all, and you can enjoy your work without having to compete against others for a living.

Summary

Knowing exactly how you add that value will give you some certainty in your working life. Because you are You-nique, once you understand the value that you add, you have a greater level of control over what work you do, and how. New working methods like fractional jobs can allow you to manage the balance between your work and the reason you do it.

Ensuring your working experience is positive plays a big part in loving your work. Creating respectful and pleasant work environments, getting the right balance between right-brain and left-brain processes, having a deep understanding of what is important to you and how you 'tick', and using experiences to learn and grow will all help to create a fulfilling and meaningful working life.

And more than anything else, making a living doing work you love requires – and inspires - enthusiasm and passion for, and in, your work.

So above all, have FUN!

And finally the B I G questions ...

What do you really feel about your work?

Where can you improve how you feel about it?

Who can help you to do that?

When are you going to ask them?

How could you add the most value to the world through your current work?

Resources

Declaration: the author has a financial interest in some of these recommended products and services, and some links are affiliate links upon which the author is paid a commission.

The financial benefit is not the reason for me giving the recommendation, it's the reward – see "P" for "Pay".

The resources listed here are those specifically mentioned in the text. You can find many more on my websites at **www.AndrewHordercom/www.Joyful-Genius.com**

Whenever I find a service, a product or a concept that I think will help people to find joy in their work, I add it to one of the websites, so do take a look there – I will probably have added more since writing this book.

Opportunity Matrix™

Created by the author, this is a deceptively-simple method of determining which of your portfolio of possibilities to focus on, to identify the core opportunities and activities that you love and will produce your success. Available as a DIY online tool, or a choice of facilitated programs.

www.opportunity-matrix.com

Email: info@opportunity-matrix.com

Core Process

Find out what it is that you are doing when you are at your very best, when you are truly 'alive and alight', when you are totally in your flow. A facilitated journey involving story-telling and deep reflection, each session takes between two and four hours, and you end up with a simple two-word phrase that acts as your talisman, your compass, your touchstone of how to re-main you at your best.

www.AndrewHorder.com/Core-Process

Email: CP@Joyful-Genius.com

Neuro-Linguistic Programming

Not as scary as it sounds, NLP is a way to identify and change negative behaviours and limiting beliefs that don't serve your objectives. That can range from behaviours like procrastination to limiting beliefs about money or success – NLP can be a very powerful way to deal with the issue. For a simple one-off issue, you could go to a Master Practitioner - each person has different needs so I suggest you ask your network for recommendations or Google "NLP" and the specific issue you want to fix.

Or you might prefer to become a practitioner yourself - many successful business owners, managers and salespeople have studied NLP. There are great many NLP courses, of varying quality – I trained with Christopher Howard's Academy of Wealth & Achievement.

Resources

Wellspring of Success

Coach and Hypnotherapist Trevor Emdon has created a self-hypnosis programme, including an audio MP3 and a work-book, to help you get into that wonderful mindset of having a confident, clear and certain belief that you will achieve success at anything you set your mind to. It wasn't until I downloaded the Wellspring of Success that I determined to start this book, and I haven't looked back!

www.AndrewHorder.com/Wellspring

Inspired Entrepreneurs (now Born To)

Inspired Entrepreneurs (now known as Born To ...) is a London-based community of entrepreneurs and would-be entrepreneurs in the Spiritual arena created by author, speaker and coach Nick Williams to support those looking for greater meaning in their work. Each month, Nick invites different speakers to give their unique take on being Born To do something. Members get access to the recording of each month's talk, so even those who can't get to London can benefit, and there is also an online forum on Facebook. The meetings usually cost around £20, which often includes a signed copy of the speaker's book, if they have one.

There are two levels of community membership – London Community membership includes a regular monthly meeting where Nick shares his ideas and members support each other in becoming successful Spiritual Pros. There is also a Global Community membership, specifically designed for those too distant to get into London regularly.

Nick has been a significant influence in the development of my work, and I heartily recommend the community if you want to create the career or the business of your dreams.

www.andrewhorder.com/born-to

Wealth Dynamics

Created by Singapore-based entrepreneur and trainer Roger Hamilton, Wealth Dynamics is a profiling system that helps business-people understand their easiest path to success. Based loosely on the i-Ching, Wealth Dynamics highlights eight main profiles, each of which plays a different role in the success of a team or a business, and only by finding a role that fully utilises your main profile can you be truly fulfilled in your work.

For moment information:

www.AndrewHorder.com/wealth-dynamics

Myers-Briggs Type Indicator (MBTI)

The most popular profiling system in the world, with some two million assessments done each year, the personality inventory was originally developed by Katharine Cook Briggs and her daughter, Isabel Briggs Myers. The MBTI emphasizes the value of naturally occurring difference in preference and is useful for understanding the type of work you are most likely to be "comfortable and effective" doing, to quote the originators.

There are a large number of companies offering online MBTI assessments, and you should definitely select one that includes a consultation to help understand the output. These vary significantly in quality and price, and you can arrange one at AndrewHorder.com where we use only highly experienced consultants – more here:

www.AndrewHorder.com/resources/mbti-profile

DISC

The assessments classify four aspects of behaviour by testing a person's preferences using word associations. DISC is an acronym for:

- Dominance – relating to control, power and assertiveness
- Influence – relating to social situations and communication
- Steadiness – relating to patience, persistence, and thoughtfulness
- Conscientiousness (caution, compliance) – relating to structure and organization

Like MBTI, there are plenty of companies offering online assessments, and like MBTI, I would suggest you find one that also includes some consultation on interpreting the results. Again, we can provide the test, using only experienced consultants – see the DISC page:

www.AndrewHorder.com/resources/disc-profile

Belbin Team Roles

Created by Dr Meredith Belbin, the team roles allow you to understand how you fit into a team. In some respects they complement Wealth Dynamics, though they are really more concerned with team effectiveness than individual effectiveness, in my view.

I did the Belbin inventory in the 1990's when I was at a large multinational corporation and found it very useful there. I found it less useful in a more entrepreneurial environment – in my view Wealth Dynamics is best for that.

www.belbin.com

Coaching from Andrew Horder

I have developed a number of coaching programmes to help people step into the joy in their work.

Core Being is currently the flagship programme, taking you through a number of intensive one-to-one sessions to uncover your unique genius that lies at the core of your being, and then show you how to access it and approach your work from that place of ease and joyfulness that means that sharing your gift with the world is simple and profitable.

From Stuck to Unstoppable is designed for those who are finding it difficult to break through a certain income or results level. We blow away the unconscious blocks that are secretly sabotaging your success and establish a strategy to create on-going momentum with a feeling of ease and joy.

Take Back Your Life is especially for those who are finding that demands on them exceed the hours available in a day, week or month. Through a number of relatively simple exercises we establish rules for prioritising based on your personal values and objectives, that mean that you are able to focus on the work that you can complete successfully and sustainably with (you guessed it) ease and joyfulness.

You probably already know which one is best suited to you – but let's have a chat about it any way.

You can book direct into my diary here:

www.AndrewHorder.com/book-chat

About Andrew Horder

Married to Daniela, Andrew lives in a small town in Surrey, right next to Gatwick airport. He finds that very handy for travel, for holidays and especially for short breaks – he has been known to take a trip to Venice just for lunch (and Daniela once took him to Bratislava for a birthday day out).

Following successful Retail, Account Management and General Management careers in both corporates and SME's, he decided to do his own thing several years ago. After an initial focus on Key Accounts Strategy - getting businesses focused on working most effectively with their best clients - that eventually morphed into getting management teams and individuals focused on their best opportunities.

Andrew's "Core Process" is *Encouraging Potential*, and he loves to make sure that everything he does is aligned with that purpose. His Wealth Dynamics profile is fairly centred, but with a definite tendency toward the analytical Accumulator.

The kind of people Andrew works best with - as in, adds the most value to - are uncontrolled entrepreneurs, the type who never stay focussed on one project long enough to really make a go of it, and who are constantly flitting from one thing to another, and back again, getting more and more frustrated as they spin their wheels and don't quite manage to make progress on any of them.

Not to mention the frustration felt by their partners (business and life), employees and accountants!

Andrew sees his role as "holding onto the kite strings". A kite can reach incredible heights with a deft touch on the strings, but if left to its own devices it quickly goes out of control and crashes to earth.

The same is true of full-on entrepreneurs - with a little discipline and a light touch on the controls, they can really fly, exceeding even their own expectations. And the first step is understanding what they do best, and what really makes their heart sing.

More recently, Andrew has shifted his focus to what he describes as 'conscious businesses' – those that approach commerce with an understanding that we are all in this together, and we will not solve the problems of the world with the same level of thinking that created them. He finds particular joy in working with conscious healers, therapists, coaches and trainers who have a real gift the share with the world and deserve to be properly rewarded for it.

To contact Andrew see the next page.

Contact Andrew

Web: **www.Joyful-Genius.com**
                                  www.AndrewHorder.com

email enquiries: **AZLW@AndrewHorder.com**

Phone enquiries: **+44 (0)20 8144 2423**

Twitter: **@joyful_genius**

Skype: **andrewhorder**

LinkedIn: **uk.linkedin.com/in/andrewhorder**

Facebook: **www.facebook.com/andrewhorder1**

Notes

[1] *Csikszentmihalyi, Mihaly: 'Flow: the psychology of optimal experience', 1992*

[2] *This introduction is a paraphrase of the words of Trevor Emdon, Hypnotherapist and coach, in the introduction to his "Wellspring of Success" audio (see resources)*

www.ingramcontent.com/pod-product-compliance
Lightning Source LLC
Chambersburg PA
CBHW070254190526
45169CB00001B/411